Made in the
USA
Monee, IL

14143852R00056